THE
RULE
OF
MORE

by Paul Holland

ISBN 978-0-9854972-5-5
Published by:
the SWG Group Fairfield, NJ
The Rule of More copyright © 2015 by Paul Holland
All rights reserved, no part of this book may be used or reproduced in any manner without the express permission of the author.

Dedication

*To everyone
who has tried and
fallen flat on their face –
then picked themselves up
and jumped again…*

FORWARD

It was more than forty years ago that I first read "The Power of Positive Thinking" by Dr. Norman Vincent Peale and the book had a profound effect on me. Since then I have read the works of countless others, attended seminars and listened to a host of speakers on the elusive topic of success.

While I walked away with something each time, there always seemed to be a piece of the puzzle that was missing. I felt like I was trapped in the old folk tale, "The Blind Men and the Elephant" where six blind men are given an opportunity to "see" an elephant by touching a different part, the trunk, the ear, the tusk… etc. Each gets to "glimpse" part of the whole creature but walks away believing he knows the whole story. The greatest problem with ignorance is that by definition, you don't know when you don't know something. After decades of wrestling with the question, I tripped over the answer one day.

Like most great discoveries – it was cleverly hidden in plain sight. I call it - The Rule Of More.

Welcome.

The Rule of More

Everyone wants more.
We want more happiness,
more wealth,
more peace,
more recognition,
more security,
more opportunity…
the list goes on.

And everyone gets more – BUT –

Often what we get more of
looks more like this:
more poverty,
more stress,
more injustice,
more frustration,
more misery,
more hopelessness…
that list goes on too.

The reason is simple.
The result is inevitable.

A Question of Inertia:

Isaac Newton was instrumental in establishing the basis for modern physics. Among his many contributions were his Laws of Motion, the first of which describes inertia.

"An object at rest tends to remain at rest and an object in motion tends to remain in motion, unless acted upon by a force."

The Rule of More applies this same basic concept to the human condition and states:

> *"You will get more of whatever you are getting now, unless something changes."*

That is because "Human Inertia" is a function of our attitudes, habits and resulting behaviors. If they are attitudes, habits and behaviors of success, we greatly increase the likelihood of that outcome. If we cultivate habits and behaviors of mediocrity, complacency and the like – that result is virtually assured. But the most interesting aspect of the Rule of More lies in the last three words, <u>unless something changes</u>.

It is in those three words that success and opportunity reside.

The first point in consideration is that, of course, "Change Happens." Over 25 centuries ago Heraclitus the historian said, "The only constant is change." We live today in an era of headlong, constant change. It is said the sum total of human knowledge now doubles every 18 years and that rate is accelerating.

In short, the force you need to affect change in your life is always present – however – the overwhelming majority of people see change as something that happens to them, rather than converting it into something that happens for them.

Truly successful people take this a step further to actively become agents of change and in the process go about creating the conditions which favor them and you can, too. This is achieved through the power of the habits we develop and the behaviors they give rise to. Either your habits will serve you or you will serve them – there is no "third option", and remember, the longer a habit remains in place (good or bad) the more force that is required to dislodge and change it.

A Predictable Disparity

In 1864, Vilfredo Pareto wrote an economic treatise entitled "A Predictable Disparity in the Distribution of the Wealth of Nations". It is commonly referred to as the 80-20 Rule.

In short, what he found was that the majority of wealth is held by a minority of the population. Interestingly enough, this principle has shown itself to have much broader application. For example; 80% of your sales come from 20% of your products – 20% of your people do 80% of the work, etc. The actual percentages will vary but the concept of the disparity does not. Many people are aware of this rule, but often fail to take it to the next logical step. Look at the 20% that holds 80% as a "Stand alone population". That means that 20% of the 20% holds 80% of the 80%. In other words, 4% of the population holds 64% of all the wealth and that in turn means 0.8% would control just over 51% of all material wealth, theoretically. Reality is not far off.

In fact what we are seeing today is the existence of twin whirlpools, the haves and have-nots. As I write this, 41% of the Earth's capital wealth is held by only 0.7% of its population. That whirlpool becomes increasingly concentrated while its counterpart, the 99.3%, expands to engulf the balance of people. The rich get richer, the poor get poorer… or in terms of the Rule of More – one group gets more wealth, the other more poverty, more complacency…

We need to stop blaming people who are successful and seek instead to understand them. The majority don't exist in mediocrity and failure because a minority kept all the success to themselves and wouldn't let them have any. Quite the contrary – it is based on a simple premise. *Success is not a function of what you have. It is a function of who you are.*

> My success or failure is not a function of your success or failure.

Why does this happen? What do they know that I don't know? What do they do that I don't do? With the answers to those questions, I have an opportunity to emulate their habits and behaviors and in the process – improve my odds of success. After all, if I want to play better golf I watch great golfers and try to copy their swing. If I aspire to be a great surgeon, I want to operate at the side of those doctors at the top of their craft to learn and duplicate their techniques. Doesn't it make perfect sense to examine how successful people approach success? Rather than be jealous, I am thankful they created a path for me to follow.

And what follows here, is an examination of some of their most important habits, behaviors and attitudes.

The Fibonacci Sequence

Leonardo Fibonacci lived in Pisa, Italy from 1170 to 1250 AD. He is considered to be one of the most talented mathematicians of the Middle Ages. He is best known for identifying the arithmetic progression that bears his name, also called the Golden Mean.

Like the Rule of More, it was hiding in plain sight but this simple ratio forms one of the most commonly reoccurring forms in nature, a graceful spiral.

The ratio is obtained by adding the last two numbers in the sequence to obtain the next number.

For example:

The sequence begins with the number 1.

1 + 0 = 1 (0 precedes 1 in the sequence)

1 + 1 = 2 (1 precedes 1 in the sequence)

2 + 1 = 3 (1 precedes 2 in the sequence)

3 + 2 = 5 (2 precedes 3 in the sequence)

5 + 3 = 8 (3 precedes 5 in the sequence)

From here the sequence begins to expand rapidly. 1, 1, 2, 3, 5, 8 now becomes 13, 21, 34, 55…

This commonly occurring spiral form in nature can also be used to describe the insidious nature of habit and behavior in ourselves. The longer we continue in a habit the more deeply it becomes ingrained and more force is required to dislodge us and allow us to move in a new and beneficial direction.

Consider the habit of smoking cigarettes. If you smoke a pack a day – you are engaging in the same habit 20 times every day. That is 7300 times a year. In 10 years, you will have engaged in the same action 73,000 times. The physical addiction to nicotine is insignificant compared to overthrowing the inertia of that volume of ingrained behavior.

That is why the best way to rid yourself of a destructive habit is not to quit "cold turkey". It is to replace it with a different, beneficial habit. For example: If you are trying to lose weight rather than eating lunch at your desk, take a 20 minute walk.

If our habits do not serve us, we are doomed to serve them. There is no third option.

Be Decisive

The first (and I believe most important) habit that successful people must develop is the ability to make decisions.

The overwhelming majority of people avoid decisions. In fact they avoid them like the plague and there are reasons why which we'll see appear throughout this book. But first let's look at why the ability to make decisions is so critical.

I am not talking about the small choices that make up our everyday existence, although I know people who agonize over the lunch menu. (I am certain you know people like that too.) I refer to decisions that are meaningful and purposeful. These are invariably decisions which involve significant consequences and people don't want to be responsible if things go badly. I have noticed that when the wheels fall off the bus, everyone was against it from the start. We always thought it was a bad idea. That's why they sell so many "Don't blame me, I didn't vote for him" bumper stickers. We hear that in the wake of every election. I wonder how can candidates win, when it always seems no one ever votes for them?

Yet, when an idea winds up a homerun, it is amazing how many were always in favor of it.

That is the dividing line. Successful people are not just decisive; they are capable of purposeful action as a result of those decisions and willing to accept responsibility for the outcomes, good or bad. (Risk & Reward – we will cover that later in greater depth.) Here's the rub – just like everything else in our lives, the more often you make decisions – the better you get at making decisions. That shouldn't come as a shock.

It is one of the most powerful aspects of a leader. People willingly follow those who are decisive because they can hang to the rear. The decision maker is a scapegoat if things go badly but the crowd is right there with them if things go well. So leaders adsorb the risk. At first blush that would seem a pretty good argument NOT to make a decision but exactly the opposite is true. If you do not, you are doomed to be a slave of circumstance, incapable of independent action. Not making a decision, leaves you at the mercy of those who do.

> NO DECISION is a decision.

It is important to note that "NO DECISION" is a decision. For example, millions of people who can vote choose not to and in the process they cast a vote. Their "vote" is to give carte blanche to the government. Do whatever you wish, double my taxes, send me to war... I have no opinion in the matter. (But remember, I will be able to display one of those – I didn't vote for him bumper stickers later.)

Just in case you still think "NO DECISION" is relatively harmless, consider the real costs based on one very real world model. Surveys show that 60% of undergraduates entering college are "Undecided" in their major. Perhaps that is why 50% of all students pursuing an education after high school dropout. It is certainly a chief contributor to the fact that on average a 4 year degree now takes almost 6 years. (I cannot fathom how or why you would assume a massive debt load with no idea of what you might do later to repay it but let's put that aside for a moment.) Instead let's focus on a student who starts college at a cost of $25K a year. Were they to graduate in 4 years – they would have a debt of $100K. However, because they can change their major two or three times – it takes almost 6 years on average. In this highly simplified model their debt load has increased by 50% to $150K, but wait. They have also lost 2 full years of employment. If we assume their lost wages would have been $50K per year – that means the education that should have cost $100K, now cost $250K. That also does not take into account 2 years of lost work experience that can never be regained.

Bottom Line – *there is a real cost to No Decision.*

This is where the successful person parts company with the rest. For most people, no decision is the direct result of procrastination brought about by confusion, fear and a desire to avoid responsibility.

> Procrastination has ruined more lives than drugs and alcohol combined.

The successful mind may make the decision of "NO DECISION" but it will be purposeful and committed. If anything it is an indicator in direct contrast to procrastination. It is a result of their focus and refusal to be diverted or distracted from it. That is the difference. In the case of the successful person, a decision of No Decision shortens the pathway to their goal because it is purposeful. For the majority – No Decision lengthens the pathway because it is based simply on avoiding risk.

When we make decisions, we seize control of situations. When we fail to make decisions we give situations control over us.

> I cannot control every circumstance.
> But I can control how I react to them.

That is the key. We don't live in a vacuum. I cannot stop the rain or alter the world economy to suit my whims but I can buy an umbrella - I can decide where to invest my money. Simply because I am not powerful does not mean I am powerless.

> Someone or something will control you -
> *Will it be you?*

Your ability to make a decision will answer that question and much more.

The majority of people work from the position that their decisions will go badly, and what if it does? Will it be the death of man? One of my favorite quotes comes from Harry Truman who said, "When in doubt I make a decision. If I'm wrong – I'll make another."

Historically, America has been called the Land of Opportunity. Up until colonization of this continent, the population of Europe was rigidly locked with a caste structure. Education, land ownership, occupation, economic status… a person's ability to change station was nearly impossible. The New World was a clean slate. Opportunity existed here as never before but it required a decision and sacrifice. Successful people understand that <u>the decisions we make, make us. They make us into the people we are and the people we are not</u>.

It is that power of decision that converts us from a person of inaction into a person of action.

Ultimately, your ability to make purposeful and committed decisions, accepting responsibility for the consequences of your actions is the first step to improving your odds of success. You cannot be an agent of change without being decisive and responsible for your outcomes.

Decisions are the crucible in which the future is cast and your future starts now.

Think

Institutes around the world tell us that we use only 5 to 10% of our brains. It is far worse than that, because I fear we only use them 5 to 10% of the time. Be brutally honest with yourself. How much of your day is spent in mindless pursuits? We live our lives on autopilot.

How often have we heard the chorus of, "What were you thinking!" When the obvious answer is - *we were not*. The very nature of our lives tends this way. Our day to day existence becomes routine, and we gravitate to that because it is "familiar and safe". We will habitually seek our comfort zone (no matter how uncomfortable it might be). Like the old saying goes, we stick to the devil we know.

Barring some malady, people are born with the ability to think, just as we are born with the ability to walk or speak. But we don't know how to do these things. We must learn how to walk and speak and THINK. They are acquired skills.

> "That which is used develops. That which is not used, wastes away." Hippocrates

What many fail to recognize is that the mastery of thought is like a razor and must be honed constantly to maintain its edge. Once dulled by misuse and neglect – it is that much more difficult to regain its sharpness and today it is more difficult than ever, consider the following:

1. Technology advances so quickly today that it seems to make everything you know obsolete on almost a daily basis. So what you learn pales in significance to how you learn.
2. The Holy Grail of technology is to make everything user friendly, to reduce or eliminate the learning curve but then we don't learn anything.
3. So learning is the best way to keep up with advances in technology and technology conspires to prevent us from developing the very learning skills that would help us the most.

> We shape our tools and our tools shape us.

We question why the United States has slipped so far behind other countries in math and science. I think that it is due in good part to devices like the calculator. It has taken away an important mental discipline. That ability has become atrophied. We point to our schools and say, we need more technology. I think we need less. It is scarcity that encourages creativity and industry, plenty does not. If anything, abundance encourages waste and complacency.

> The worst thing you can give someone is a diploma, because they think they are done learning.

The development of your mind, of the habit of thinking begins with:

Learning. People will ask me, "Learning what?" To which I say, everything. Become a sponge. The universe is alive with unanswered questions. We should burn with curiosity. For everything we know there are trillions and trillions of things we don't know. Develop an insatiable thirst for facts and ideas. Don't restrict it to one topic or field. Because the more bits of information you accumulate, the more something greater starts to emerge. One of the reasons we think in lock step is because we never move outside of area of expertise and view our tiny world as part of a greater universe. It is not enough to go deep, we should also seek ways to widen our frame of reference. Thinking should broaden our minds – not confine them. Once we do that, we start to recognize:

Patterns. How things fit together. The more pieces of the puzzle you have, the more you begin to see how they can be combined. One of the most brilliant minds to grace America was Richard Feynman, Ph.D., tenured professor of physics at the California Polytechnic Institute and Nobel Prize laureate. When the Challenger space shuttle exploded, he is the person NASA turned to and the one who figured out why. He gave us back a pathway to the stars. He said about himself, his talent lay in the ability to recognize patterns. This ability to see how things interconnect is critical to the creative process and to the third leg of this tripod:

Problem Solving: As we see patterns evolve we can place them over the top of real world problems and look for points of convergence and the "holes" in our thinking. The goal is to evolve solutions for crying needs. That is where opportunity hides in plain sight. That is finding your true value. Many people create problems. Many more stand back and watch hopelessly saying what can I do? *You can do.* The ability to solve problems sets you apart from the field. The more problems you solve, the facts you learn and the wheel turns again.

Woody Allen once said that 90% of success was just showing up. He was going for the gag but he may not have been far wrong. Consider what it might mean if you dedicated part of your day, every day, simply to the practice of focused and directed thought. Develop the habit of honing your mind, becoming more insightful. How much farther ahead from the crowd do you suppose you might be?

Stop looking at what things do and start looking at what they make possible. Here is where it becomes critical to success.

> The eyes see what the mind looks for.

I mentioned earlier that the majority of people walk through life on autopilot, wondering why they always seem to miss the brass ring while the same few always get there first. The reason is that an acute mind is always looking for the missing pieces to the puzzle even while they may be concentrating on something completely different. They see opportunity everywhere while their less fortunate brethren step over it. In fact the overwhelming majority have been conditioned by the constant and numbing onslaught to our senses to tune out the world and our fellow beings. Continuous over stimulation has desensitized us. Reliance on our tools has weakened us. There is no app for success and the grave difficulty that everyone faces is that when you are not thinking, your habits take over. If you have developed the habits of success – the likelihood is that you will be alright. However if you have developed the habits of mediocrity, complacency and failure – that is precisely what you will fall back on.

If we expect to take value from the system, we must bring value to the system and that means being a problem solver.

Need I say more… Just Think.

> Two of the most common blueprints for failure are to:
>
> Act without thinking
>
> - and to -
>
> Think without acting.

Goals

I am certain we have all heard it a thousand times, about the necessity of setting goals for ourselves. I doubt you would find too many people who would disagree with their importance after all - a man with no destination invariably gets there.

Which begs the question, why do so few people have goals for themselves? I'm not talking about a standard response like, "Someday I'll be on a beach somewhere…" or performance benchmarks that may be imposed (usually by others) in our professional lives such as a sales or production quota. I am talking about the absence of personal goals.

I have seen different studies that suggest only 4 out of 10 people even bother to make New Year's resolutions anymore and of those who do only about 8% see them through. About half don't survive the first 30 days but that is because they were not really goals to begin with. For the most part, they would barely qualify as suggestions. For example: I will lose weight is not a goal. But "I will lose 2 pounds a week for the next 3 months" is a goal because it is both reasonable and quantifiable. We'll address that in some greater depth shortly.

First, I believe it is more important to appreciate WHY goals are so hyper-critical to our success as individuals. The reasoning is simple.

Goals exist only in the future, they are a vision of what we want to occur. To be an agent of change, isn't that exactly where we need to be? We need to define, as precisely as possible, what that change will look like if we hope to make it into a reality. It is more than simply growth or movement. The goal is purposeful, directed, quantifiable growth and movement.

The overwhelming majority are driven by events rather than goals. But events have already occurred. They are beyond our ability change. I cannot influence what has already happened – I can only be influenced by it and the more attention I give to it, the more influence and control it will exert over me. By choosing to dwell in the past and present –

people willingly surrender their ability to craft their own future. Successful people understand this.

> Nothing I do can alter the past.
> Everything I do – changes the future.

I cannot un-ring a bell, I cannot un-speak a word but every corner I turn, every action I take or fail to take alters the passage of time. It is our goals that act a litmus test to keep us pointing toward our true north. That is why goals are much more than things we would like to achieve or acquire. They shift our focus from things we cannot change and keep our eyes locked on what we can change. Henry Ford said, "Obstacles are those frightening things we see when we take our eyes off the goal."

Our goals give us purpose and direction. It is about much more than what we do, it is about why we do it. That provides us with a deeper level of understanding. As a result we think more, our decisions are more considered and focused. This is another reason why they are so valuable. In the absence of goals you cannot hope to become an agent of change.

If we accept the premise that goals are essential to our success, why are we so reluctant to set them for ourselves? There are really only two possible explanations. The first is that we are completely satisfied with our lot in life. There is nothing we could possibly wish to change or improve… Okay, there is really only one possible explanation.

There is a powerful quote from the televangelist and motivational speaker, Robert Schuller who said, "What would you attempt if you knew you could not fail?" What if we reverse that for the overwhelming majority and ask, "What are you reluctant to attempt because are afraid you will only be disappointed?" I believe that most people have simply had our dreams and goals beaten out us. Establishing a goal requires that we have some expectation we can reach it. Whether we choose to admit it or not, if we do not try – we cannot be disappointed. So, we "aim low". We adopt the habit of complacency.

The result is that *you will get more of what you are getting right now – <u>because nothing ever changes</u>*.

The habit of setting and pursuing goals, invites change. In fact, it demands change. Let's look at how we go about beginning that process.

First good goals must be achievable – or you are simply setting yourself up for disappointment. You are "proving" they don't work for you and that is the last thing you want when trying to replace an old destructive habit with a new beneficial one. You may wish to start small but your goals should be graduated so that they grow as you do. A goal must be challenging. They should be constantly stretching and testing your limits. Success itself then becomes a habit and a process. By doing this success is not something we achieve – it is something we maintain – a different way of life.

We also need to recognize that goals are paid for cash up front. You have to put the effort in before you can expect a return. Your boss doesn't hand you a paycheck first thing Monday morning and ask you to try and get a lot done this week. The farmer doesn't get paid for his crop before he clears and plants the field.

All that having been said – if you will have to sacrifice for your goals and put the effort in before seeing any kind of a return – shouldn't your goals be worthy?

Build the habit of setting and pursing goals. There is no free lunch. Expect to work and sacrifice to make them into a new reality and even as they are realized, replace them with the next challenge. Make them worthy of your efforts and you won't be disappointed. Each plateau will be more rewarding than the last and your new habit will become addictive.

Plan

Successful people plan – most people just react.

Sadly it makes perfect sense. If the majority of people are focused on events they cannot plan, by definition they can only react. They have no other choice. They must accept whatever circumstance drops in their laps and try to make the best of it. Does that sound uncomfortably familiar?

That is not to say that everyone can't be taken by surprise. No one is immune. But when the unexpected happens, having a plan in place gives us a foundation, a frame of reference to enable our recovery much quicker. It helps minimize our losses. Sometimes it can even be turned into help us achieve success faster. That is because we knew where we were, where we were going and how we were getting there.

> When things go badly – get back on the path.

In the absence of a path, you are doomed to wander and when things go awry, you are completely without direction. You are a ship that is out of sight of land without a chart or compass – completely at the mercy of the wind and waves. Not a very promising prospect.

We already looked at and agreed to the necessity of establishing goals in our lives. If we know where we are now and the goal tells us where we want to be – a plan is the direct line that connects the two. By definition a straight line is the fastest and most efficient route between two points. It simply makes sense.

Our plans do several important things.

First: They help us identify and inventory the resources we will need to reach our objective. How much will it cost? How long will it take? Do I have or can I access the necessary skills, capital or other resources that I will need? If I don't have one or more of these elements – how can I go about getting them?

Second: The plan enables us to prioritize our efforts and resources. Doing things out of sequence wastes your time and other valuable resources. You can't put a roof on until the walls are up. You can't erect the walls until the foundation is in place... This is an area where people often waste one of their most valuable resources needlessly, their reputation. Why would you invest your time, money and talent with someone who is constantly taking two steps back for every one step forward? Your most profitable path is the one where things happen in their most efficient order. A good plan lays out that time line.

Third: A plan exposes deviation. It contains milestones and go/no-go points to make certain you are not going astray. The goal is to reach the goal with the straightest line possible, but we live a real world. Things happen. (I cannot control all circumstances.) When things happen the plan should contain sufficient flexibility that I can correct my course based on what those things are. (I can control how I react to circumstances.)

Fourth: A plan is a sanity check. Is it possible? Is it practical? Does it fit with the other things I am doing or will it cause me to sacrifice other more worthy endeavors? Will the results I can reasonably expect be worth the price this will exact from me? Not all opportunities are created equal. Simply because I own a shovel does not mean I want to acquire mineral rights on the moon.

The existence of a plan does not guarantee your success – it does however greatly improve your odds. It does so because it gets us thinking, examining alternatives, looking at contingencies and it requires us to keep thinking about. Goals place us in the future – plans keep us moving in that direction. The two are integrally linked, purpose and action.

Plans do much more than just to show you the next step in the path. We don't live in a vacuum. We are not immune to circumstance but we can evaluate their effect and make choices. Sometimes things happen to knock us off the path. When it does – go back to the plan. Is it intact, does it still make sense? Learn from what occurred and keep going or modify it accordingly (and keep going).

> Momentum is your best friend,
> until you sit down.

That is why plans need to be organic and like any other living thing – you need to make their proper care and feeding, a habit.

Work

> The harder I work, the luckier I get.
> Thomas Jefferson

As I write this, there are almost 1,400 Billionaires in the United States. There are more than 9.6 million Millionaires.

The overwhelming majority will get up every day and go to work. Why - if they don't need the money?

> Successful people don't work for money.

Conversely, almost 150 million people get up every day and go to a job just for a paycheck. Millions more have sold their future by being trapped within the vicious cycle of handouts that grips our society. Today more than half the population receives some form of government assistance, without realizing just how expensive a free lunch truly is. We sell our prospects for pennies on the dollar and think we are beating the system. Nothing could be further from the truth. What a waste of human potential. Consider the following paradox:

If money is an indicator of our worth and value AND if money can be gotten for free... What does that say about the value of money, or us?

> The ugly truth about a system of entitlements is this: We are not giving you this because you are special and deserving – We are giving you this because you can't make it on your own... It increases dependency rather than encouraging us to become self-reliant. Entitlements inhibit us from ever realizing our true potential.

This is the myth that the overwhelming majority buy into; they tie their sense of self-worth to the size of their paycheck. It is a ridiculous and self-defeating system.

Here is the proof; people who work for wages think they are underpaid. The people who pay those wages think you are overpaid. The outcome of such a system is easy to foresee. People are marginalized, bullied, resentful, jealous, unappreciative... and why should anyone be thankful – after all I paid for it, I worked for it – I deserve it. In fact, I deserve more… Sound familiar? What people do not realize is that more is exactly what they are getting. It is just not the "more" they want.

Money is just something we use to keep score. The true currency today is information. Every person has intrinsic value, because they know things I don't know, but we overlook that because of the clothes they wear or the car they drive.

Every day I hear people tell me about how much they hate their job and if you do, the answer is to love your work instead.

Work is the cradle of success because in ways nothing else can, it provides us with countless opportunities to collaborate, set goals, solve problems, learn new things, to challenge our abilities. The list of benefits is almost endless *and they pay you too.* It is a remarkable deal when you think about. The trick is simple. Stop counting other people's "money". That is the fastest road to unhappiness I know. Instead, focus on increasing the value you bring to the table. That is your opportunity to shine, to stand out.

> Success is not the result of making money –
> Making money is the result of success.
> Earl Nightingale

Successful people create value and the system compensates them for the value they create. In other words, the Rule of More gives them more but they are paid in the currency they value. This is why someone like Mother Theresa, who lived in abject material poverty, was so profoundly successful in spiritual terms. She just counted wealth by a different yardstick.

> Stop thinking in terms of money.
> Start thinking in terms of value.

Conversely, the drug dealer, crooked politician or scam artist may have lots of money – but it is acquired through the misery of others. I would hardly consider them successful, would you?

In the "entertainment age" in which we live, people glamorize the rich and famous, all too many of whom wind up in the clutches of addiction and depression. But aren't drugs and alcohol a way to escape your situation? How ironic.

Ultimately the dividing point goes back to "Someone or something will control you. Will it be you?"

Successful people are in control, they are "the boss" of themselves, regardless of whether or not they "have a job" or are self employed – they are self-directed. The majority of people have a "paycheck mentality". If you occupy the corner office and stare at the clock hoping for 5 o'clock on Friday afternoon – you are a wage slave no matter what your job title may be. If you are still there two hours after closing because the job isn't done to your satisfaction yet – you are the boss of you.

The mantra of today's average man seems to be, Do as little as possible – take all you can. But that is what makes them and keeps them average.

Consider one last point. As an example, look at someone like a truly great athlete, or a gifted musician. Their natural ability gives them that 5 or 10% edge that sets them apart from the field. But that natural ability would be squandered if they simply sat back and never practiced. The 90% that brings the top within reach is made up of hard work, dedication and sacrifice.

That having been said – if you could play golf or baseball 90% as well as a professional athlete – If you could play the violin or piano 90% as well as a professional musician… do you think others might be impressed at your performance?

Love your work and let your true value shine.

Independent

Successful people think and act independently. That goes without saying. They are willing to buy when others are selling and vice versa. They are not different because they are successful. They are successful because they are willing to be different and that is not as easy as it sounds because -

The overwhelming majority of people conform.

This shouldn't come as any great shock. After all, we are social creatures. That is our nature. The desire to group together is burned deep within our animal brain. There are any number of creatures out there that are faster and stronger, better at swimming or climbing. We lack big sharp teeth and claws. We don't have quills, venom or wings. All we have are our wits and each other. Yet, still we sit at the top of the food chain. Society itself couldn't exist with some measure of conformity by definition. But like so many other things in life it is a double edged sword, because it discourages creativity, initiative, ingenuity – in short all those "extras" that make you stand out. People often belittle intelligence when logic says we should be applauding it.

> Every advancement in human history required someone to think differently.

Since the dawn of man, adversity caused us to huddle closer together. Don't break from the herd. That is where the danger is. In ancient history, banishment was considered to be far more cruel than execution. Today, look around you - cliques, gangs, tribes, clans… call them what you will. It is all about who is in and who is out. It doesn't matter if it happens in the school lunch room or the board room, our lives are run by politics and pecking order. Rejection, ridicule and exclusion are some of the bully's most powerful weapons. In order to survive, we go along. We comply.

In the process of doing that, the first thing we sacrifice is the power of decision. The first key to becoming an agent of change is the very first thing we cast aside. Because making a decision makes us different, by definition.

Because it is such a engrained survival habit – we don't even realize we are doing it and look at the real cost. We sacrifice the very habits of success we have been addressing here. Instead, in order to conform we inherently mimic the behavior of the majority of people who dwell in poverty, mediocrity, worry and frustration. That is why, as Henry David Thoreau said, most men lead lives of quiet desperation. They dream of being more and dare not because of what others may think or say.

In choosing the path of the non-conformist, what does the successful person really risk? Are we are afraid that we will no longer be allowed to live in misery and despair? We'll have to find someplace else to live. (I'm okay with that.) We will have to endure the ridicule of people who censure creativity and look down their noses at those who are different. (I can live with that too.) After all why would I place so much value in the opinion of people who have no respect for my opinion?

> Don't worry about leaving misery behind.
> They always have lots of company.

One of the healthiest ways to view the necessity of "taking the path less traveled" (Thank you, Robert Frost) is to see yourself as a trailblazer, demonstrating to others there is a better way and that there is more than enough room for them to join you. In adopting and cultivating the habits of success you are in a way providing a public service.

Perhaps one of the oddest paradoxes is the concept of how competition and collaboration fit into this puzzle of conformity versus independence. Strangely, the great majority in the process of enforcing compliance will employ competition as a lever. "Who can conform the most?"

You would think that a society, where its survival depends on collaboration, would be employing that aspect of our nature instead but it doesn't work. That is because belonging to the group is not driven by the desire to work together, but rather a complex competition to gain acceptance. It is the pecking order that takes precedence, that drives the majority to "out conform" one another. In its worst case, it is how storm troopers and fanatics are forged.

> It is not safety we find in numbers.
> It is poverty and a degradation of the spirit.

To successfully break from the herd requires an understanding of fear, because fear is the greatest of all human motivators. I say that because it is not an emotion. It is a physiological response. A willingness to walk away from the perceived security of others is directly contrary to our genetic hardwiring and it is scary. Here is something that will help.

> When fear stands before you – it holds you back.
> Put fear behind you and it drives you forward.

Either you master your fears or they master you. There is no third option. However, having mastered your fears you will have the ability to draw on their strength. That is ultimately the difference between the hero and the coward. Both are afraid but one uses fear to his advantage by converting an enemy into an ally.

Get comfortable with being a group of one. Sadly the road to pursue success is often lonely but that does not mean you are alone. You are merely connected differently.

Failure

Failure is neither good nor bad, it is merely necessary. It tells us where the boundaries are. Everyone fails. What sets successful people apart is that they learn from it.

> Success is not the absence of failure.
> It is the absence of quitting.

Yankee fans in recent years revered Derek Jeter who had a lifetime batting average of .310. That means he failed to get a hit 69% of the time. I have never heard of a golfer who turned in a final score of 18, for 18 holes. Have you?

Yet we equate failure with losing and for that reason, the overwhelming majority permit fear to steal their potential. I was a volunteer scout leader for over twenty years. I once had a mom ask me what my job was in that capacity. I replied, "My job is to make sure your son doesn't hurt himself... badly." As part of the maturation process, I expected young men to cut their fingers, burn their dinner or tumble out of a canoe. In the process they would also learn how to apply a bandage, how not to cook chicken and the indescribable joy of having an extra pair of clean, dry socks.

> Most of our failures result because
> we never learned how to fail.

Today, people go to extreme lengths to prevent their children from failing. I was appalled years ago when a friend of mine was describing how his then young son participated in playing tee ball. There were no outs, no innings, no score was kept. In our zeal to eradicate losing – winning had to be thrown on the fire. How does that prepare you for life?

I am told that the third leading cause of death among young people aged 15 to 25 is suicide. That age range coincides with young people being out on their own for the first time. I don't think that is a coincidence. They have no idea how to handle disappointment, loss and failure. I ask you, who goes through their life without ever experiencing disappointment, loss and failure? No one gets to do that. It is inevitable.

Young people today have more powerful tools and fewer constraints than ever before. That is a dangerous combination. Failure simply tells us where "NO" starts. That is why it is absolutely essential. Failure is inevitable – success is not.

> If you learn something – it isn't failure.
> It is just an object lesson.

There is a famous old story about Thomas Alva Edison being asked if he had really failed 10,000 times while trying to make the first light bulb. His reply of course was that he had not failed – but that he now knew 10,000 ways how not to make one.

What would have happened if he refused to learn from his first mistake? What if instead he wasted time trying to blame others, to make excuses, to rationalize and defend his decisions… despite 10,000 failures – he might have passed away in relative obscurity still be clinging to the one error he couldn't admit and we'd all be searching for a candle. We are all fallible.

> If you have to rationalize your actions –
> They probably were not rational to begin with.

When we make a mistake, it is not a sign of weakness but in this crazy, over-competitive world we live in – we think it is. So we dare not admit it. If we do learn anything it is to avoid making decisions and assuming responsibility in the future. It is directly contrary to the habits of success. If we cannot own our mistakes – we cannot own the object lessons that accompany them. That inability redirects our focus from the future we can affect more positively based upon a lesson learned. Instead we shackle ourselves to a past event we cannot change. In the process we lose our ability to channel the power of change and instead become its captive.

> Making mistakes is not a sign of weakness.
> The inability to admit them is.

Failing to own up to our failures is in fact, another failure. Moreover, our intolerance for mistakes invariably spills over in terms of how we deal with others when they misstep. Ultimately it leads to the establishment of a culture of fear where people are reluctant to experiment and think independently. It holds everything back. I much prefer the approach of Fiorello LaGuardia, who served three terms as mayor of New York and was quoted as saying, "When I make a mistake – it's a beaut."

Our mistakes my not all be beautiful – but they are our own and as such they are part of the pathway that makes each of us into each of us. If we accept the premise that all people possess intrinsic value, based upon their knowledge – failure should be recognized as one of the most important aspects of our journey here. You can only learn through experience. It may be your own or that of someone else, but if we were to allow our fear of failing freeze us where we stand and the advance of all human knowledge would cease. People would stop trying to learn because they might not "get it" immediately. In many ways - failure is more important than success, but only when we learn the lessons it teaches.

If you wish to embrace your successes – you must also be willing to embrace your failures.

Because all of them, good or bad, are the direct result of the decisions you make and the actions you take.

The only true failure is not to learn from our mistakes.

Successful people know this.

Value

The majority of people focus on what things cost and as noted earlier, they do this in the absence of clearly defined goals. As a result they tend to disassociate the natural cause and effect of risk and reward.

Successful people see the two as integrally linked. For that reason, they do not fear risk – they simply analyze it and balance it with the potential return. They are looking at the value of a thing rather than merely at the price tag.

> "I never buy a building because I want it,
> I buy it because it is under-valued."
> Donald Trump

It follows the same principle as work, the concept that value should be the natural outcome of effort, sacrifice, ingenuity and industry. It is about paying the price.

> Everything has a price –
> but not everything has a return.

What many fail to recognize is that the cost of a thing may only be a fraction of the true price. For example, what if your company could use a new machine that had the ability to cut production time in half? The actual purchase of the machine is only one part of the equation. Its true value can only be ascertained when amortized across its potential contribution to the bottom line over the course of time.

The same holds true for any asset or activity. Your education, capital, personnel and most important your time – because time is the only thing you have that cannot be replaced.

It makes sense, if we accept that scarcity and availability drive the value of any commodity, what could ever be more valuable than time? This is one of the great dividing lines between success and mediocrity. The purchase price of "a thing" always requires that you spend time, in addition to whatever else that thing may cost. If you need a computer, a vehicle, a building, a hammer… If you need to hire a person, or take a seminar… before you spend a dollar – you invest time. But by agonizing over the dollars, we spend more time than we have to in the process and as I pointed out earlier – you can get more money, but you cannot get more time.

Successful people look at the total cost, the total risk and the anticipated return and make a decision at the outset whether or not the result is worth the price before they get drawn in.

> Go back to the goal – the plan,
> that is the litmus test.

In addition, because successful people build performance milestones into their plans, they have the ability to see if their original expectations are being met. Is it taking too long? Is it costing too much? Is it diverting too much attention from your core activity? Has the expected return shrunken, perhaps due to changing circumstances? Ideally, they have the maturity to cut their losses. Therein lies the value of two of the quotes cited earlier, Mr. Trump, "I never buy a building because I want it..." and President Truman, "When in doubt I make a decision, if I'm wrong I'll make another." The first recognizes that value based decisions are not clouded with emotion – it makes it far more difficult to make an honest assessment of all the factors. It also makes it more difficult to cut ties and make "another decision" when indicated.

DNA

All living things on Earth are amazingly complex. They convert energy, grow, mature, respirate, reproduce, consume, heal, eliminate waste… Higher order organisms move, think, collaborate, communicate, learn… We don't think about it because it is just our nature, billions of cells working in harmony, automatically. We don't have to give it a conscious thought.

Because at the heart of all that is DNA, the blueprint of life as we know it. Basically, DNA (deoxyribonucleic acid) is a sugar molecule. It inhabits almost all of the cells of your body. (Except red blood cells which have no nucleus.) Although it is normally all coiled up, if it were stretched out straight it would resemble a ladder. In fact the DNA from one cell of your body, if uncoiled would be about seven feet long.

The "rungs of that ladder" are made up of only four compounds; adenosine, thymine, cytosine and guanine (abbreviated A,T,C,G) which combine in pairs. Adenosine will only link to thymine. Cytosine will only link to guanine. Those pairs can read right to left or left to right, but those few simple combinations placed in order along the length of the DNA molecule contain all the information that make you into the unique being you are. This simple "chemical computer" not only governs all we have in common, it establishes our planet's rich diversity of life. When you consider that you have 75% of your DNA in common with a pumpkin, it is truly a remarkable thing.

Success and failure each possess their own DNA and as you might expect they are mirror images of each other.

The four Pairs look like this:

SUCCESS	FAILURE
ID	OD
OF	IF

The first set of pairs stand for Inwardly Directed and Outwardly Directed.

Successful people are Inwardly Directed. They are self-determinate, the masters of their own fate. They achieve this through the power of decision, conscious thought, establishing goals and planning the steps necessary to attain them. They own all their outcomes – accepting responsibility for the consequences of their actions and inaction, both good or bad. They learn from mistakes (both their own and those of others) and having adsorbed the object lesson in that experience - let them go and move forward.

> You can't dwell in both the past and future.
> You must choose.

Conversely – the DNA of failure leaves us Outwardly Directed, under the control of external forces. These people live lives of mediocrity, complacency and failure because they are controlled by circumstances. They hate their jobs. Desperation, stress and regret gnaw at them. They deny themselves a future because they cannot let go of the past. They are doomed to follow because they fear the consequences of decision and therefore cannot lead. In short they relinquish control. How can you hope to succeed if you are not in control?

Instead, they rely on things like luck and hope which are not very effective strategies. They react rather than act. The difference is that reacting, by definition happens after the fact. You will always be a step behind, relegated to picking up the broken shards and pieces left in the wake of others.

The second set of pairs stand for Outwardly Focused and Inwardly Focused.

The DNA of success is outwardly focused. The successful mind is allocentric. Such a person has the ability to see how the pieces of the puzzle fit in relation to each other, independent of themselves. This ability to view things from a remote perspective enables you to make better decisions based on a more complete view, with less emotional influences. Better decisions, grounded in more complete information, on average will yield better outcomes. When we are outwardly focused, we start looking at the consequences of our actions longer term. We start seeing how the ramifications of what we do affect a broader landscape. Outwardly focused people are looking at success as a process , not a series of events. They also recognize that a rising tide floats all boats. It doesn't do any good to be the strongest branch on a dead tree. That is why the successful mind seeks common pathways that enable others to share in the fruits of success because the Law of Association and the collaborative model it supports will continue to bring you even more.

On the opposing side – the Inwardly Focused person is principally only concerned with themselves. They are egocentric, only capable of seeing things in terms of how they relate back to them.   They are the center of their own universe.   The result is as you might expect. They seize short term gains at the expense of the future. They are worried about this month's sales figures, their next paycheck, while successful minds are planning five years out. The inwardly focused person tends to be more highly competitive and as a result isolated.   In the process they limit their options and resources. They cannot admit mistakes and try to deflect responsibility.   This makes them reluctant to be decisive and take the lead although they will gladly hang on to the coattails of success as it goes past.

> A dog thinks everything else thinks like a dog, because that is all they understand.

The inwardly focused person thinks everyone else is also egocentric. For them the golden rule is: do unto others before they do unto you. Isn't it fascinating that when you fire someone, it is just business but when you get fired – it is very personal. That is the egocentric mind.

It is not a question of good or bad – right or wrong…

This is the world that we have created, a world governed by the Rule of More and the Law of Association.

I cannot change it – but I can change me and thereby alter my outcomes.

No Guarantee

Many people will tell you that your success is governed by karma or some secret law of the universe, but I do not believe that. Theologians have debated for centuries why bad things happen to good people (and vice versa). It is not like a bank account or a ledger where you can store up credits, debits and IOU's. There is something far more basic at work though, rooted firmly in human nature, which I will explain shortly.

First, however, it must be clearly understood that no is guarantee of success. We live in a time when everyone thinks they are entitled, and when things don't break in their favor - you generally hear an outcry of, "It isn't fair..." Strangely, I have never heard anyone say that when things did go their way.

No one can guarantee you success because there will always be circumstances beyond our control. There are bad people out there who are governed by human frailty such as greed, jealousy, prejudice, stupidity. There is no magical force to overcome that, which is why there is not, nor can there be any guaranty of reciprocity. Simply because you help or serve someone does not mean they obligated to return the favor. But just as there are bad people, there also good ones - others who practice the habits of success. That is why it is critical to recognize that both sides exist.

Simply because you "do it all right" does not mean your success is assured. It merely means you did it right. (By the way, in my opinion, holding true to your principles does make you a success.) But investing the energy to develop the habits of success can dramatically improve your odds. General Douglas MacArthur said, "Chance favors the prepared man."

It is like picking the exact right card from a deck. If there are 52 cards, your odds of success are 1 in 52.   If you are just trying to pick an ace, your odds are 1 in 13. If you only need a face card, 3 in 13 or any card from a particular suite, the chance of your success would be 1 out of 4. The more you develop strong habits of success, the more variables or circumstances you take off the tables – the better you control the odds. Every person has the same opportunity to win and the same opportunity to lose. There are too many variables, despite what your broker or bookie may tell you – there is no "sure thing". Unless of course there is something nefarious going on but that just proves my point. You can do it all right and still come up short because the "game has been rigged" and you are on the outside.

> Truly successful people -
> don't leave success to chance.

Here is a good example. Many years ago while working in the exhibit industry, I received a frantic call from a client. I had saved them from potential disasters on a number of occasions but this one was really a major challenge. My office was in New Jersey. They were setting up for a show in Georgia, scheduled to open in less than two days. A forklift had dropped a crate and smashed their custom reception counter and two custom podiums. They needed them replaced, renting something was not an option – they insisted they must have the material replaced before the show opened. We pulled the plans and fabricated two new podiums and a multi-level reception counter as replacements that day. All of it was disassembled and packed flat in three flat cardboard boxes and that night a courier service flew them to Georgia. I packed up some tools and a change of clothes and caught the last flight to Atlanta where I rented a van and picked up my own freight. After driving to the exhibit hall, I carried each of the three boxes in on my back and rebuilt the pieces right there on the show floor before it opened. Needless to say – the client was elated, but that was not the end of the story.

Less than 90 days later, I received a call from that same customer to inform me that they had purchased another company who stored their exhibit assets in Tennessee where it was cheaper. They asked that we ship all their material in storage down there – in short, we were fired.

When I have related that story to people they will sometimes respond by saying, "I'll bet you never do that again for a customer." To which I say, "Of course I will and I have. I didn't go to those extremes because of who they were – I did it because of who I am."

> Someone or something will control you.
> Will it be you?

This is why persistence is so important. You must remain true to yourself in a world where reciprocity, ethics and fairness are often lacking. You must hold your course in the certain face of failures, disappointments and setbacks.

> I cannot control all circumstances -
> but I can control how I react to them.

Which bring us to the true power behind that process.

The Law of Association

The Law of Association goes beyond that and consists of three points:

FIRST - Things that are alike attract one another. Whether you are conservative or liberal, intellectual, creative, athletic, socially conscious, environmentalist or apathetic - don't you prefer the company of like minded people? We seek out those who are like us, who value what we value. It is engrained into us, the need to belong, to associate within a clan, a tribe, a clique... Man is a social animal. It is the herd mentality. That is why we gravitate toward that center and draw comfort from it. The group validates our beliefs and opinions, no matter what they are. We must recognize that first, driven by that need to associate, we will unconsciously move toward that which is "comfortable" even if it is not what is in our best interest and that includes finding others just like us.

But to succeed, we need to be willing to be different.

SECOND - We become more like that which we associate with. If you spend all your time with creative people, becoming more creative is a natural outcome. If you spend all your time with intellectual people, you will engage in more and more intellectual pursuits. Sports, books, movies, games, rituals – it doesn't matter what binds the group together. What matters is that to be a fully engaged member your participation is mandatory. Your adoption of their core value set is required in order to gain entrance and remain there. By definition, deviation from the standards, conventions, the rules of order are cause for exclusion. That can be crushing. So we "go along to get along". In fact, over time our personal identity is sacrificed and in its place we adopt the persona of the groups to which we belong instead to describe and define our existence. The longer we do that, the more deeply habits and behaviors become engrained.   We dehumanize ourselves to fit in.

THIRD - Over time the First and Second points create a cycle of reinforcement and refinement. It is obvious on its face. The more we spend time with a group, the more we practice their rituals and behaviors. In the process we adopt their core value structure. The further we move in that direction, the more we attract others with the same mindset… It is a self-fulfilling prophesy.

It is the Rule of More, human inertia.

However, understanding the existence of the Rule of More enables us to employ the Law of Association to alter our direction by exercising the power of decision.

Enacting Change

The Rule of More states:

You will get more of whatever you are getting now, unless something changes.

The Law of Association states:

1. Things that are alike attract one another.
2. We become more like that which we associate with.
3. Over time the First and Second points create a cycle of reinforcement and refinement.

We began with the premise that most people fail to make a decision and by doing so surrender their outcomes to circumstances. Circumstances brought about by the decisions of others. But by exercising the power of decision we can consciously choose with whom we associate. In the process of doing that, we can reject the habits and behaviors of mediocrity and instead build and reinforce those of success by making them a part of our daily lives… Excellence is therefore an option open to all of us.

It is important to remember that people are like cake. Every cake has the same basic ingredients, flour, eggs, sugar, etc. That makes them all the cake but they come in all different kinds, shapes and sizes because the quantities of those ingredients are varied, other things are added… That is what makes them different. People are all the same in that we hope, fear, love, envy, aspire… but to different degrees. That is what makes us all individual. A good person can commit a bad act. A bad person can perform a kind act. This concept is important from two standpoints. First that it affords each of us the ability to change because we all possess the basic building blocks we need. Second, it tells us that over time what a person truly values will make itself apparent. Gravitate to those values you would like to see in yourself.

We can best become an agent of change, when we start by changing ourselves for the better.

It is about inertia. Momentum builds over time. The longer we practice a habit or behavior, the more difficult it is to modify it. That is why the future starts right now.

> Nothing you can do will alter the past.
> Everything you do affects the future.

Do not underestimate the power that these associations can have. How many times have we heard the old adage, "One bad apple spoils the barrel"? We worry about our kids "running with the wrong crowd". We say things like, "It isn't what you know – it's who you know."

The best way to "break a habit" is to replace it with another. The trick is to make that new habit beneficial. That is why your success is fueled by the establishment and maintenance of a Strategic Network of Alliances.

> **YOU ARE EITHER NETWORKING**
> **– or –**
> **YOU ARE NOT WORKING!**

The two common mistakes in the creation of building a truly effective Strategic Network of Alliances are:

First, we network exclusively within our comfort zone. Bankers only talk to bankers, engineers talk to other engineers… <u>Likes Attract</u> but then there is no the fresh exchange of information.

> We learn more from people who are different.

Further, we tend to stay within our socio-economic strata. If I want to become a person of high net worth, don't I need to associate with those kinds of people too? How else will we learn from them? Break down barriers. No one will do it for you. You must get comfortable with being uncomfortable. It is all part of paying the price.

Second, a true strategic alliance is never unilateral. It must be based on mutual benefit, in the principles of cooperation. Both parties must profit. You are probably thinking; "Wait a minute, if I want to associate with successful, high net worth individuals what could I have that they would want?" A very natural question best answered by the relationship between Napoleon Hill and Andrew Carnegie. On the surface they were polar opposites, the "Steel King" and the "kid" but only if you measured them with the same yardstick. Hill sought fame and fortune. Carnegie had that to burn. What Carnegie wanted was an empty vessel to fill with the legacy of his philosophy of success. He could not have given that away to one of his millionaire friends could he? They wouldn't take it without interjecting their own slant on things. It was the disparity of their stations in life that made the match.

How do you bridge the chasm to begin such an association?

There are two things you must do.

First, stand out from the crowd by becoming a person of interest. Read, study, and develop successful habits such as industry, acuity, insight, vision, focus, initiative, interpersonal skills… The more you do along these lines the further you will remove yourself from the masses. Sadly most people fear power including their own greatness. Instead they choose to remain cloaked in obscurity. There are those two of nature's most common defenses again – camouflage and the safety of the herd.

Most people fear appearing on the radar of powerful people. Successful minds covet that position.

Second, fish where the fish are. Organizations, associations, seminars, meetings… but i*t is NOT about stalking people*, which will only lead you into trouble. The best way to make someone run away is to chase them. It is simply about positioning yourself to win. When you do that, when you display the qualities that make you attractive - others will choose you. Things which are alike, attract.

If you wish to become noticed – make yourself into someone worthy of note and don't hide your light under a basket. The means to accomplish this is to develop and practice the habits of success. Sadly, in a world governed by the Rule of More, the majority inherits more and more mediocrity and complacency – the average is continually being driven down. While unfortunate for them, it is easier and easier for you to appear exceptional.

Become proficient in the art of Empowered Asking.

Empowered Asking

People who ask from an inferior position, do not ask. They beg. The problem with that is obvious. It is the natural outcome of those who have surrendered to circumstance.

People who ask from a superior position do not ask. They command and sometimes demand. Here the problem is not quite so easy to see, but it can create jealousy, animosity and resentment.

Empowered asking occurs when we seek to level the field.

Let's look first at when you might be in a position that could be considered inferior. You build your case before approaching the other party. Establish a sound train of reasoning as to why it is in the best interest of everyone to come to a common conclusion. Demonstrate in concrete terms the value that you are bringing to the table and keep it very positive. Either the other party will accept this value or they will not. Remember there is no guaranty of reciprocity and there is no assurance that they will see value (or logic) the same way you do. If they see things differently – listen to their side of the argument, but don't argue. They may have some additional compelling insights you hadn't considered. As a result, you might wish to reconsider your position. If that is the case, don't be afraid to say so. It demonstrates maturity and wisdom. You may also find that they are simply unmoved by reason. In short, they don't care. They are unreceptive to your position. If that happens, you have only two options walk away or give in to whatever they want.

If you are asking from might be construed as the "superior" position going in – everything I said above still applies. Because if you take the time and invest the energy to win over the hearts and minds of others they will see themselves as stakeholders instead of underlings. It is the line between being a boss and a leader, the difference between having people work for you because they must and having people work with you because they want to.

Empowered asking works both ways.

Competition and Collaboration

One of the greatest impediments in getting the Rule of More working for you today is surrendering control to the myth of competition.

How often have we heard, it's a dog eat dog world. But that is just an excuse…

We love to compete. We love it because we are addicted to the adrenalin rush we get from it. That's what keeps professional sports teams and amusement parks in business. They permit us the vicarious thrill of risk, winning and losing. The driving force behind all of that is fear, specifically fear of failure.

> Winning and success are different things.
> Why win a battle if it costs me the war?

Fear is not an emotion; it is a physiological response to danger. Fight or flight – that is why our hearts race, our palms sweat, we get that knot in our stomachs… It is hardwired into us genetically. It was designed to keep us off the menu when in our distant past larger, stronger, faster creatures with big teeth and sharp claws caught our scent. Although you rarely hear about a friend, neighbor or co-worker being devoured on their way to the supermarket today, the bio mechanism to give us that jolt and subsequent euphoria of well being that follows is still alive and well.

This aspect of our nature cheats us however of understanding and appreciating what true success is. The reason that I say this is because it convinces us that success is momentary and fleeting rather than a systematic progression, a way of life. Success should be a verb, not a noun.

Competition causes us to isolate ourselves. We dare not expose weakness by asking questions or by seeking help. In the process we severely limit our growth. In the ultimately competitive model, every other person on the planet is our potential adversary, by definition because only one – can be number one. The insanity of it all is that no matter how good you are at what you do, it is an unsustainable position. The fastest man alive will eventually lose a step. The strongest among us will someday fade. Giving your life over to competition is like electing to live on the island of cannibals. No matter how good you are, sooner or later, it will be your turn in the pot.

> Competition is a drug and drugs cloud reason.

Just as we are hardwired to compete, there is a second and even more powerful drive that is intrinsic to our nature. True success is almost invariably the product of collaboration. We are social creatures. Working together is a biological imperative. Our greatest asset has always been one another.

At this point, people will often stop me and say, "Yes but what about_____?" You can fill in the blank. They will usually name some great athlete, scientist, doctor, entertainer... There are any number to choose from. But I would wager they did not develop their skills living alone on a desert island. They didn't grow up in the vacuum of space. Other people invested in them, coached them, mentored them, supported them. Sustainable success is the product of many minds and hands working toward a common goal.

Successful people understand that it is about people. Just as the ultimate competitor has billions of enemies – the ultimate collaborator has billions of potential allies. It is not a case where completion is bad. It can strengthen us and drive us forward but we need to master it or it will master us. Remember, something will control you. Will it be you?

Collaboration and cooperation are the true engines which drive society. Successful people recognize this and tap into that power to create new pathways.

By enabling others to share in success, we help ensure our own.

Last Word

The decisions we make, make us.

When we think, we act. When don't, we react because our habits take over.

The eyes will see what the mind looks for.

Learning is the key to adaptation, never stop.

A goal is our vision of a successful tomorrow.

We achieve goals through planning, discipline and hard work. Luck is a four letter word.

We must be willing to be different.

Treat success as a process; failure as an event.

Failure teaches us more than success does.

Our attitude enables us to alter our habits.

Thoughts and habits determine our behavior.

It is almost impossible to break a habit – it is much easier to replace one with another.

The relationships we form, help to form us. By choosing with whom we associate – we help shape our future.

No decision is a decision.

I cannot control every circumstance but I can control how I react to them.

Get comfortable with being uncomfortable.

Life is not fair, because too many people choose not to be. For that reason, there is no guaranty of reciprocity.

Everyone must play the hand they are dealt, we have no alternative. By understanding these things however, you can become the dealer, *an agent of change.*

Nothing you do can alter the past…
Everything you do affects the future…
That being said – your future starts now.

The direction it takes is entirely up you, master or victim. You can move to direct your own inertia or surrender to it. But either way you will get more...

So, DECIDE.
What you will do with it -
and never let someone else tell you
what your success should look like.

About the author:

Paul Holland had the uncommon wisdom to marry his best friend over thirty years ago and together they managed to raise three fine young people.

The rest, is incidental.

You may also profit from

5 Second Selling

www.ingramcontent.com/pod-product-compliance
Lightning Source LLC
Chambersburg PA
CBHW070306100426
42743CB00011B/2377